ARMY RANGERS

Simon Rose

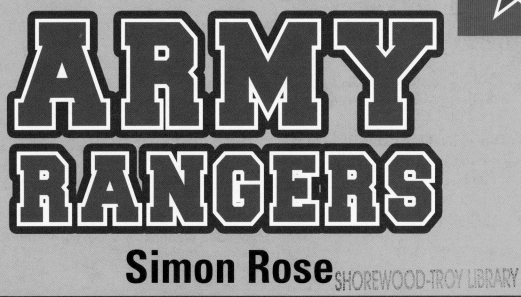

www.av2books.com

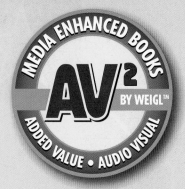

AV² provides enriched content that supplements and complements this book. Weigl's AV² books strive to create inspired learning and engage young minds in a total learning experience.

Your AV² Media Enhanced books come alive with...

 Audio
Listen to sections of the book read aloud.

 Key Words
Study vocabulary, and complete a matching word activity.

Go to **www.av2books.com**, and enter this book's unique code.

 Video
Watch informative video clips.

 Quizzes
Test your knowledge.

BOOK CODE

K145719

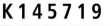 **Embedded Weblinks**
Gain additional information for research.

 Slide Show
View images and captions, and prepare a presentation.

AV² by Weigl brings you media enhanced books that support active learning.

Try This!
Complete activities and hands-on experiments.

... and much, much more!

Published by AV² by Weigl
350 5th Avenue, 59th Floor
New York, NY 10118
Website: www.av2books.com   www.weigl.com

Library of Congress Cataloging-in-Publication Data
Rose, Simon, 1961-
 Army Rangers / Simon Rose.
   p. cm. -- (U.S. Armed Forces)
 Audience: Grades 4-6.
 Includes index.
 ISBN 978-1-62127-449-0 (hbk. : alk. paper) -- ISBN 978-1-62127-455-1 (pbk. : alk. paper)
 1. United States. Army. Ranger Regiment, 75th--Juvenile literature. 2. United States. Army. Ranger Regiment, 75th--History--Juvenile literature.
 3. United States. Army--Commando troops--Juvenile literature. I. Title.
 UA34.R36R67 2014
 356'.1670973--dc23   2012040422

Printed in the United States of America in North Mankato, Minnesota
1 2 3 4 5 6 7 8 9 17 16 15 14 13

022013
WEP301112

Project Coordinator: Aaron Carr
Designer: Mandy Christiansen

CONTENTS

WHAT ARE THE RANGERS?

The 75th Ranger Regiment, also known as Rangers, is a special operations group of the United States Army. The Rangers are an **infantry** unit and carry out most of their operations on land.

The Rangers are one of the two main groups under the Army Special Operations Command (ASOC). The U.S. Army Special Forces, also know as Green Berets, is the other main ASOC group. ASOC is part of the United States Special Operations Command (USSOCOM). The Department of Defense is in charge of USSOCOM and all branches of the Armed Forces except the Coast Guard. The Secretary of Defense is the head of this department. The president of the United States is the commander-in-chief of the entire Armed Forces. The Rangers have about 2,000 members on active duty.

★ All U.S. Army Rangers attend Ranger School. This is one of the most challenging training courses in the U.S. Armed Forces.

USSOCOM Organizational Structure

MARSOC

JSOC

ASOC

AFSOC

NSWC

Green Berets

75th Ranger Regiment

PROTECTING THE COUNTRY

The 75th Ranger Regiment protects the United States and defends its activities and interests around the world. The Rangers work with other U.S. special operations groups and other branches of the Armed Forces in times of war. In peacetime, they are always prepared to take action wherever they are needed.

The 75th Ranger Regiment has three main special operations **battalions**. Each of these battalions takes turns at being the Ranger Ready Force (RRF). The RRF is the first battalion called on when Rangers are needed. They and the other Ranger battalions must be ready to go anywhere in the world within 18 hours.

On the Front Lines

In battle, the Rangers are mainly involved in operations on the ground. They also may use aircraft and ships to attack the enemy. Their specialized missions against enemy forces include airborne attacks, raids, capturing enemy airfields, and rescue operations for U.S. military personnel and important equipment. Rangers have taken part in U.S. military operations in many parts of the world.

THE RANGERS MOTTO

The 75th Ranger Regiment's official motto is *Sua Sponte*. This is Latin for "Of Their Own Accord." This is because Rangers volunteer three times—for the Army, for Airborne School, and for the 75th Ranger Regiment. The unofficial motto of the Rangers is "Rangers lead the way."

HISTORY OF THE RANGERS

The Rangers trace their history back to America's colonial period. Rangers fought in wars between the colonists and Native Americans in the 1600s and 1700s. Rangers also fought in the American Revolution, which led to the United States becoming an independent nation.

1676
★ The first Rangers are formed during King Philip's War

1776
★ Declaration of Independence is signed

1812 TO 1815
★ War of 1812 against Great Britain

1754 TO 1763
★ French and Indian War

1783
★ Victory over Great Britain in the American Revolution

1861 TO 1865
★ American Civil War

1776

1861

Through the years, the Army Rangers have taken part in missions around the world. They have fought in Europe, Asia, Africa, Central America, and the Middle East.

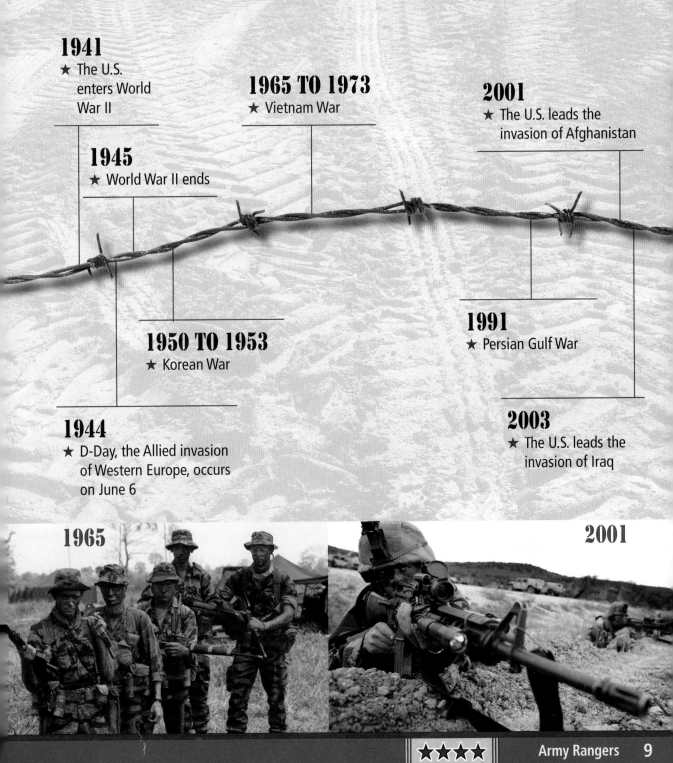

1941
★ The U.S. enters World War II

1965 TO 1973
★ Vietnam War

2001
★ The U.S. leads the invasion of Afghanistan

1945
★ World War II ends

1950 TO 1953
★ Korean War

1991
★ Persian Gulf War

1944
★ D-Day, the Allied invasion of Western Europe, occurs on June 6

2003
★ The U.S. leads the invasion of Iraq

1965

2001

RANGER BASES AROUND THE WORLD

T he 75th Ranger Regiment has bases in Georgia and Washington in the United States. In most of their missions overseas, the Rangers use the same bases as other Army units.

1 Washington

The 2nd Ranger Battalion has its headquarters at Joint Base Lewis-McChord near Tacoma. Army and Air Force bases were merged in 2010 to form the base, which is a training center for all the Armed Forces.

2 Georgia

The 75th Ranger Regiment has its headquarters at Fort Benning, a large U.S. Army base. Fort Benning is also the home of the 3rd Ranger Battalion and the Ranger Training Brigade. The 1st Ranger Battalion is stationed at Fort Stewart in Hinesville and at Hunter Army Airfield in Savannah.

3 Panama

In 1989, all three of the Rangers main battalions took part in the U.S. invasion of Panama.

4 Grenada

In 1983, the 1st and 2nd Ranger Battalions were involved in the invasion of Grenada.

ARCTIC OCEAN

NORTH AMERICA

United States

PACIFIC OCEAN

ATLANTIC OCEAN

N W E S

SOUTH AMERICA

Scale:
621 Miles
0   1,000 Kilometers

SOUTHERN OCEAN

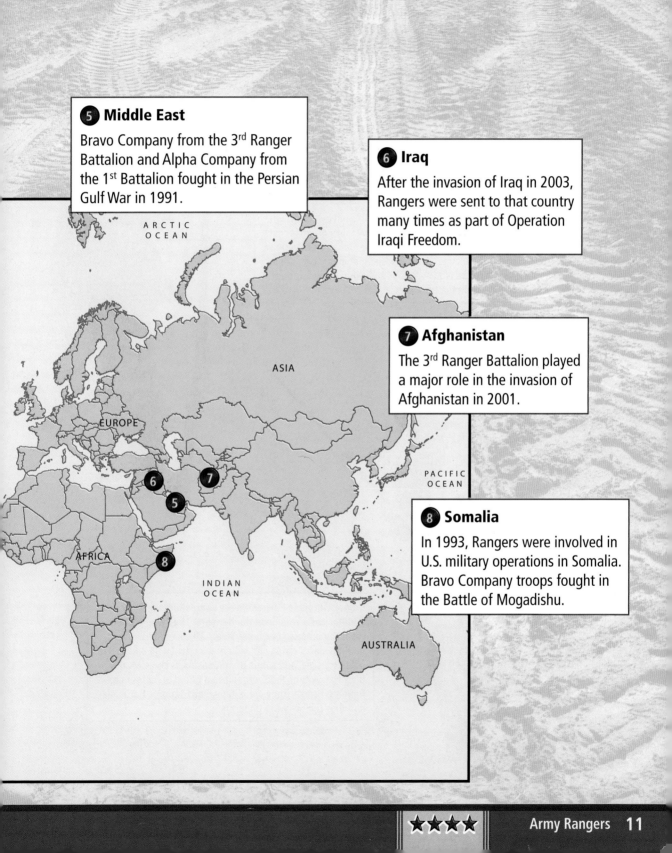

5 Middle East

Bravo Company from the 3rd Ranger Battalion and Alpha Company from the 1st Battalion fought in the Persian Gulf War in 1991.

6 Iraq

After the invasion of Iraq in 2003, Rangers were sent to that country many times as part of Operation Iraqi Freedom.

7 Afghanistan

The 3rd Ranger Battalion played a major role in the invasion of Afghanistan in 2001.

8 Somalia

In 1993, Rangers were involved in U.S. military operations in Somalia. Bravo Company troops fought in the Battle of Mogadishu.

ARCTIC OCEAN

ASIA

EUROPE

PACIFIC OCEAN

AFRICA

INDIAN OCEAN

AUSTRALIA

RANGER UNIFORMS

In the 1600s, Rangers usually fought in **civilian** clothes. They began to wear uniforms in the 1750s.

FRENCH AND INDIAN WAR

Rogers' Rangers was a colonial force recruited by the British to fight in the French and Indian War. They wore green jackets and **Scottish bonnets** made of wool. Waistcoats, wool or linen shirts, leggings, and moccasins were sometimes worn. Some Rangers dressed like Native Americans when living for long periods in forests on the frontier.

AMERICAN REVOLUTION

Daniel Morgan's Riflemen were **sharpshooters**. They were another early version of the Rangers. They would often wear the clothing of frontiersmen. This included fringed hunting shirts, hats with wide brims cocked up on the left side, trousers, and shoes or moccasins. Francis Marion, the "The Swamp Fox," organized a group of Rangers to fight the British. They were known as Marion's Partisans, and they did not wear uniforms.

WORLD WAR II

The M1 helmet was made of steel with a plastic and fabric liner. The helmet protected the wearer from **shrapnel,** but it did not stop bullets.

Rangers wore U.S. infantry uniforms in World War II. The jacket came down to the upper thighs. It was made of windproof cotton and was a drab green color. The jacket also had a detachable hood, drawstring waist, two large pockets at the chest, and two lower pockets.

The trousers were made out of the same material as the jacket. Leggings covered the top of the shoes and trouser bottoms. They kept the trousers from snagging on **barbed wire** or branches.

The helmet is made from a bullet-resistant material known as Kevlar or Twaron. Goggles protect the eyes. A night-vision device can be attached to the helmet for operations at night or in low-light conditions.

TODAY

Today, Rangers wear the Army combat uniform in the Universal Camouflage Pattern. This blends tan, gray, and green and works effectively in desert, woodland, and urban environments. The Improved Outer Tactical Vest, or IOTV body armor, can be worn over the jacket.

The trousers have two storage pockets at the thighs and two pockets at the calves. Soldiers wear tan-colored combat boots. They also use elbow pads, kneepads, and gloves.

RANGER WEAPONS

Rifles and handguns have always been the main weapons used by the Rangers. Modern Ranger rifles are lightweight, powerful weapons used throughout the U.S. Armed Forces.

AMERICAN REVOLUTION

Pennsylvania Longrifle
The Pennsylvania Longrifle had a greater range than most **muskets**. This meant that the marksman could remain hidden and select a specific target rather than fire at a large group of soldiers. However, the rifle could not be fitted with a **bayonet** and it took longer to load than other rifles.

CIVIL WAR

Colt Revolver
Mosby's Rangers were often involved in close-range combat in the American Civil War. Rifles were not the best weapons for this kind of fighting. These Rangers used a Colt **revolver.** The gun had a rotating cylinder that could hold six bullets. It had a range of up to 100 yards (91 meters). Rangers constantly practiced their shooting with the revolver.

WORLD WAR II

M1 Garand Rifle

The M1 Garand was one of the main guns used by Rangers during World War II. It was a **semiautomatic** rifle. Each time the trigger was pulled, it fired a single bullet. When empty, it then ejected the clip holding the bullets. The M1 was reliable and accurate. However, it made a loud sound when the clip ejected. If the enemy heard this sound, they knew that the Ranger was out of ammunition and needed to reload the gun.

TODAY

M4 Carbine Rifle

The M4 carbine rifle is one of the main guns used by the Rangers today. It is a shorter and lighter version of a similar gun, the M16 assault rifle. The M4 can be fired in several ways, including semiautomatically and in three-round bursts. It operates on gas. Its barrel is 14.5 inches (37 centimeters) long. The short barrel allows soldiers to use the rifle better in tight spaces.

JOINING THE RANGERS

Anyone wishing to join the Rangers must first join the Army. People applying must be U.S. citizens or permanent residents. They must also be at least 18 years old, have a high school education, and be able to pass the Army Physical Fitness Test (APFT). Some Ranger positions may have other requirements. A college degree is needed to qualify for **officer** training programs. Women are not allowed to join the Rangers.

Applying to the Army

Step One: Apply to the Army online

Step Two: Talk to a recruiter about the Rangers

Step Three: Take the Armed Services Vocational Aptitude Battery (ASVAB)

Step Four: Visit the Military Entrance Processing Station (MEPS)

OATH OF ENLISTMENT

❝ I do solemnly swear that I will support and defend the Constitution of the United States against all enemies, foreign and domestic; that I will bear true faith and allegiance to the same; and that I will obey the orders of the President of the United States and the orders of the officers appointed over me, according to regulations and the Uniform Code of Military Justice. So help me God. ❞

Boot Camp Basic Combat Training for Army recruits is often called Boot Camp. This nine-week training program turns civilians into soldiers. After completing Boot Camp, soldiers move on to Advanced Individual Training (AIT). In AIT, they learn the skills they need for a specific Army job. Airborne School is a three-week program that teaches basic parachuting skills.

The Ranger Assessment and Selection Program (RASP) is the final test for Ranger trainees. It consists of an eight-week course that involves extremely tough physical training. Many recruits drop out during RASP. Ranger School, a 61-day course, is a requirement for all who wish to become officers.

JOBS IN THE RANGERS

Being an Army Ranger is not just about serving in combat. There are many types of careers in the Rangers. There are jobs in engineering, business, communications, electronics, medicine, vehicle maintenance, and working with computers and technology. The training and experience gained in the Rangers can also lead to successful careers in civilian life after military service is completed.

Construction and Engineering

Engineers in the Army Rangers specialize in many different areas. There are a variety of jobs in construction, such as carpentry, electrical work, and plumbing. Other jobs include designing barriers against the enemy, working with maps and charts, detecting mines and other explosives, and maintaining vehicles and other equipment.

Communications and Technology

Jobs in this field include computer programming, **military intelligence**, electronics, and technical support. Communications experts in the Rangers work with a wide variety of communications equipment, from basic radio communications to modern satellite systems.

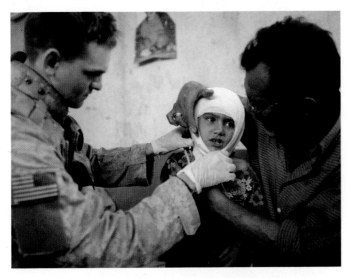

Health Care and Medicine

Careers in health care and medicine include working as doctors, nurses, dentists, and audiologists. Other jobs involve managing health care facilities, laboratory research, and operating medical tools such as X-ray and ultrasound equipment.

RANGER COMMUNITY LIFE

Life in the Rangers is much like civilian life. Rangers work regular hours at a job, they spend their time with their families, and they fill their free time with hobbies, sports, and other activities. Some personnel live in barracks, but others live in houses either on or off the base.

Many bases where Rangers are stationed have all the facilities of most towns and cities. This may include hospitals, schools, day care centers, libraries, sports facilities, and shopping malls. The 75th Ranger Regiment provides a wide variety of programs to improve the quality of life for families living on military bases. These include counseling services, programs to improve on-base education and job opportunities for family members, and programs that help families deal with the stress of having a parent working in a combat area overseas.

★ Rangers must be ready to leave their families with little notice.

WRITE YOUR STORY

If you apply to join the Army and the Rangers, you will probably need to write an essay about yourself. This is also true when you apply to a college or for a job. Practice telling your story by completing this writing activity.

1 **Brainstorming**

Start by making notes about your interests. What are your hobbies? Do you like to read? Are you more interested in computers or power tools? Then, organize your ideas into an outline, with a clear beginning, middle, and end.

2 **Writing the First Draft**

A first draft does not have to be perfect. Try to get the story written. Then, read it to see if it makes sense. It will probably need revision. Even the most famous writers edit their work many times before it is completed.

3 **Editing**

Go through your story and remove anything that is repeated or not needed. Also, add any missing information that should be included. Be sure the text makes sense and is easy to read.

4 **Proofreading**

The proofreading is where you check spelling, grammar, and punctuation. You will often find mistakes that you missed during the editing stage. Always look for ways to make your writing the best it can be.

5 **Submitting Your Story**

When your text is finished, it is time to submit your story, along with any other application materials. A good essay will increase your chances of being accepted, whether it be for a school, a job, or the Army Rangers.

TEST YOUR KNOWLEDGE

1 Which weapon did sharpshooters use in the American Revolution?

2 What was the main weapon used by Rangers in World War II?

3 What is the RASP?

4 Where is the headquarters of the 75th Ranger Regiment located?

5 Which Rangers are based at Joint Base Lewis-McChord?

6 Which colonial force wore green jackets and Scottish bonnets?

7 How long is the Airborne School training program?

8 At what age can you join the Rangers?

9 What does USSOCOM stand for?

10 What Ranger unit played a major role in the invasion of Afghanistan?

Answers: 1. The Pennsylvania Longrifle 2. The M1 Garand semiautomatic rifle 3. Ranger Assessment and Selection Program 4. Fort Benning, Georgia 5. The 2nd Ranger Battalion 6. Rogers' Rangers 7. Three weeks 8. 18 years of age 9. U.S. Special Operations Command 10. The 3rd Ranger Battalion

KEY WORDS

barbed wire: a strong wire with twisted, sharply pointed spikes at short intervals

battalion: a military unit with 300 to 1,200 soldiers; several battalions usually form a regiment or a brigade

bayonet: a knife or sword that can be attached to the end of a rifle

civilian: a person who is not an active member of the armed forces

infantry: soldiers who fight on foot

military intelligence: information about the armed forces of another country

musket: an early version of the rifle, developed in the 1500s

officer: a soldier in a position of authority

revolver: a handgun that contains a revolving cylinder with several chambers for holding and firing bullets

Scottish bonnet: a brimless cap made of wool

semiautomatic: a gun that can fire a round of bullets and load a new round each time the trigger is pulled

sharpshooter: a highly trained rifleman who shoots at the enemy from concealed positions or long distances

shrapnel: pieces of metal that fly out of a bullet or bomb when it explodes

INDEX

Log on to www.av2books.com

AV² by Weigl brings you media enhanced books that support active learning. Go to www.av2books.com, and enter the special code found on page 2 of this book. You will gain access to enriched and enhanced content that supplements and complements this book. Content includes video, audio, weblinks, quizzes, a slide show, and activities.

AV² Online Navigation

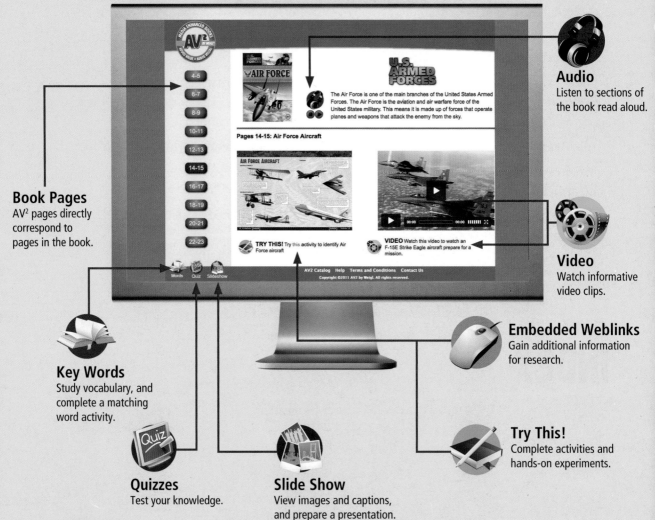

Audio
Listen to sections of the book read aloud.

Book Pages
AV² pages directly correspond to pages in the book.

Video
Watch informative video clips.

Key Words
Study vocabulary, and complete a matching word activity.

Embedded Weblinks
Gain additional information for research.

Quizzes
Test your knowledge.

Slide Show
View images and captions, and prepare a presentation.

Try This!
Complete activities and hands-on experiments.

AV² was built to bridge the gap between print and digital. We encourage you to tell us what you like and what you want to see in the future.

Sign up to be an AV² Ambassador at www.av2books.com/ambassador.

Due to the dynamic nature of the Internet, some of the URLs and activities provided as part of AV² by Weigl may have changed or ceased to exist. AV² by Weigl accepts no responsibility for any such changes. All media enhanced books are regularly monitored to update addresses and sites in a timely manner. Contact AV² by Weigl at 1-866-649-3445 or av2books@weigl.com with any questions, comments, or feedback.